Balanced Meals

BY KATIE CLARK

The Child's World

Published by The Child's World®
1980 Lookout Drive • Mankato, MN 56003-1705
800-599-READ • www.childsworld.com

Acknowledgments
The Child's World®: Mary Berendes, Publishing Director
Red Line Editorial: Editorial direction
The Design Lab: Design
Amnet: Production
Photographs ©: Front cover: FoodIcons; BrandX Images; FoodIcons,
3, 6, 11, 12, 13, 16, 17; BrandX Images, 3, 4, 9, 10, 14, 18, 23;
choosemyplate.gov, 5; Kids in Motion, 7; sonya etchison/Shutterstock, 8;
Ilike/Shutterstock Images, 15; PeterBajohr/iStockphoto, 21

ISBN: 978-1623235994
LCCN: 2013931392

Printed in the United States of America
Mankato, MN
July, 2013
PA02178

ABOUT THE AUTHOR

Katie has been writing stories since she was a little girl. Now that she's grown, she spends her time reading, writing, and playing make-believe with her daughters. Katie's writing for children has appeared in numerous publications, including books and magazines.

Table of Contents

CHAPTER ONE

Three Meals a Day

It is time for a hike! You tie your shoes and pull on your pack. You have your coat, hat, and bottle of water. You are ready to go. Wait, you forgot the most important part! You forgot to eat breakfast. Before heading out the door, you grab a granola bar and a banana, and you gulp down a glass of orange juice. Now you are ready to go. You are glad you ate a healthy breakfast to give you the energy to climb the trail. Now you can finish your hike with lots of energy to enjoy it.

▲ Bananas can be part of a healthy breakfast.

▶ Opposite page: Use the MyPlate diagram to make healthy eating choices.

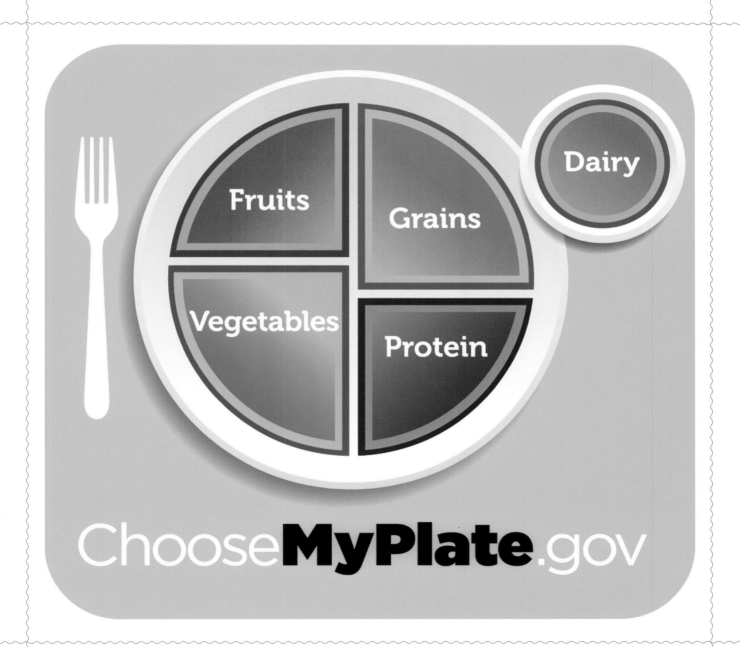

The MyPlate diagram shows the five food groups that make up a balanced meal and a healthy diet. The diagram illustrates what your plate or bowl or cup should look like at every meal. Every food group should be on your plate at every meal.

◄ Fill your empty plate with fruits, vegetables, grains, protein, and dairy.

EMPTY CALORIES

Empty calories come from foods that do not give your body many **nutrients**. Unhealthy foods are ones that have solid fats or added sugars like butter, candy, or soda. If you eat too many of these foods, you are not giving your body the **vitamins** it needs to stay healthy. It is best to eat fewer empty calories and more healthy foods.

▶ Eating healthy meals gives you energy to go for a walk with a friend.

Most people eat breakfast, lunch, and dinner. Eating breakfast gets the body started on the right foot each day. It gives the brain and body the energy they need to get going. Breakfast foods keep the body from getting tired or weak throughout the morning. Eat a good breakfast to start the day right. Lunch is the midday meal. It helps kids stay focused through the afternoon until dinner. Dinner is a good time to catch up on healthy foods in the five food groups: fruits, vegetables, grains, protein, and dairy.

Healthy eating habits keep the body strong. Eating three meals a day is part of eating well. Healthy meals help kids stay strong and give them **energy** to get through the day. Kids use energy each time they move. Walking, brushing teeth, and playing the piano all use energy. When kids use up the energy from one meal, they need to replace it with energy from another one.

Energy is measured in units called **calories**. Each calorie is a small bit of energy. Kids need energy to perform well in school, play sports, and do chores. They need it to ride bikes, go swimming, and run races. Energy comes from calories, and calories come from the food you eat. It is important for boys and girls to use the same amount of energy they take in. If you eat 200 calories for breakfast you should use 200 calories by vacuuming the floor, walking the dog, or playing ball.

▲ Take your dog for jog to burn off calories.

CHAPTER TWO

Necessary Nutrition

Eating healthy foods keeps the body strong. The five major food groups are fruits, vegetables, grains, protein, and dairy. A small amount of fat is also important for a healthy diet. Eating the right amount of these foods can keep you healthy. They will give you vitamins and **minerals**. Healthy foods keep the body working well.

Fruits and vegetables provide the **fiber**, vitamins, and minerals that help keep your body and mind healthy. These foods can help you eat

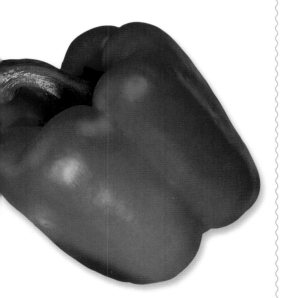

▶ **Colorful fruits and vegetables are part of a healthy meal.**

◄ Opposite page: Enjoy a cold glass of milk with your dinner.

► Make whole grains, like these rolls, a part of every meal.

▼ Eggs are a good source of protein.

more good calories and fewer empty calories. Eating fruits and vegetables can lower the chance of getting some diseases. They taste good, too!

Grains make up another food group. Like fruits and vegetables, grains give the body fiber, which helps the heart and **digestive tract**. Grains also have lots of B vitamins. These help the body make energy. Choose **whole grains** like oatmeal, brown rice, and bread. Whole grains contain all the nutrients in a grain seed.

Eating protein is also good for the body. Protein comes from meat, tofu, or soy. Protein keeps the muscles strong. It can help heal injuries, like cuts or scrapes. Chicken, lean beef, and pork have protein. Beans and eggs are protein foods, too.

The last food group is dairy. Dairy is full of **calcium**. Calcium is an essential nutrient that makes bones and teeth strong. Dairy foods like milk, yogurt, and cheese have calcium. Dairy has vitamin D, too. Vitamin D helps bones **absorb** calcium.

Oils and fats are not a food group, but they are a part of a healthy diet. There are good fats and bad fats. Good fats come from eating foods like

◄ Milk contains essential nutrients calcium and vitamin D.

VERY IMPORTANT VITAMINS

The body needs lots of vitamins and minerals to work properly. Vitamins A, B, C, and D are important for healthy eyesight, energy levels, teeth, and bones. Other important vitamins and minerals are iron, folic acid, and potassium. These help your body get oxygen to your brain, make new cells, and have a healthy heart. Eating foods according to the MyPlate guidelines can help you get the vitamins you need.

▶ Get fats through healthy oils like canola oil and olive oil.

nuts or fish. Kids can also get healthy fats from oils such as canola oil or olive oil. Bad fats come from eating solid fats like red meat, butter, and vegetable shortening.

The body needs only a small amount of fat. Get your fats from healthy choices.

CHAPTER THREE

Make Meals with MyPlate

The five basic food groups are the building blocks for a healthy body. They each offer something the body needs. MyPlate shows us how much of each food group to eat. For example, MyPlate shows us we need lots of fruits and vegetables.

MyPlate guidelines tell you to fill half your plate at each meal with fruits and vegetables. Choose apples, berries, mangos, or any other fruit you enjoy. One hundred percent fruit juice is good, too.

▲ Vegetables and fruits provide your body with the nutritional building blocks it needs.

▶ Opposite page: Have a salad and a glass of orange juice before dinner.

Vegetables are next on the plate. It is good to eat colorful vegetables like green peas, orange carrots, or red peppers. Green beans, broccoli, and squash are great choices, too. Some people like 100 percent vegetable juice, which also counts as a vegetable. Kids should eat 1 to 1 1/2 cups of fruit and 1 1/2 to 2 1/2 cups of vegetables every day.

Grains are the next portion of the MyPlate plate. Oatmeal, popcorn, pancakes, pasta, or biscuits are good grain choices. Kids need at least 5 ounces of grain a day. A half cup of cooked oatmeal,

◄ Popcorn is an easy way to eat whole grains.

Did you know water is just as important as eating healthy foods? Water keeps your body **hydrated**. This means it keeps the body from getting dried out. Water helps your blood get oxygen to your brain. It also helps vitamins and minerals reach all areas of your body. Water can take oxygen and nutrients throughout your body without the extra calories that come from sodas or other sugary drinks.

▶ Peanuts and other nuts contain healthy fats.

five whole-wheat crackers, and 3 cups of popped popcorn all count as 1 ounce of grains.

One-quarter of the MyPlate plate is filled with protein. Lots of foods have protein. Meat, soy, nuts, and beans all have it. Eggs and seafood are full of protein, too. Choose lean meats, such as boneless, skinless chicken breasts, instead of fatty meats like beef. Kids need 4 to 5 ounces of protein a day. One egg, a tablespoon of peanut butter, and a sandwich slice of turkey all count as an ounce of protein.

Dairy is the last major food group. Choose low-fat dairy products like 1 percent milk or plain yogurt. Calcium-fortified soy milk is also part of the dairy group. Kids need 2 1/2 to 3 cups of dairy every day. One cup of milk and a regular cup of yogurt count as 1 cup of dairy.

Fats should be a small part of your diet. By eating healthy foods, you can eat the right amount of fat without eating any extra. Kids should eat up to 4 teaspoons of oil a day. A tablespoon of mayonnaise, eight olives, and 1/3 ounce of peanuts all have a teaspoon of oil in them.

The MyPlate guidelines help kids cook up healthy breakfasts, lunches, and dinners. When they follow the guidelines, kids will know that they are eating enough of the five food groups to build strong bodies and minds. Try out these menus for a healthy breakfast, lunch, and dinner.

▲ **Have some blueberries at lunch and broccoli at dinner.**

Breakfast	Glass of orange juice
	Egg omelet with spinach and ham
	Two pieces of whole-wheat toast with peanut butter
Lunch	Glass of milk
	Turkey sandwich on whole-wheat bread with mayonnaise, lettuce, and tomato
	Handful of baby carrots
	Cup of blueberries
Dinner	Glass of milk
	Grilled chicken breast with olive oil and lemon marinade
	Steamed broccoli
	Rice pilaf
	Yogurt with strawberries

Hands-on Activity: Play with Your Food!

Try arranging your plate according to the MyPlate guidelines.

What You'll Need:

A plate, a glass, milk, fruits, vegetables, proteins, and grains

Directions:

1. First, fill half your plate with fruits and vegetables.
2. Then, put your protein on the remaining empty part of your plate. It should take up a little less than half of the space. Fill the last available part of your plate with your grains.
3. Last, fill your glass with milk.

Now your plate looks exactly like MyPlate!

Glossary

absorb (ab-SORB): To absorb means to suck up. Vitamin D helps bones absorb calcium.

calcium (KAL-see-um): Calcium is an essential nutrient. Calcium helps build strong bones and teeth.

calories (KAL-ur-eez): Calories are measurements of energy found in food. Kids need calories to play sports and do well in school.

digestive tract (die-JESS-tiv trakt): The digestive tract is a series of tubes that pass food through your body after you eat it. The digestive tract breaks food down into minerals and vitamins your body can use.

energy (EN-er-jee): Energy is the power to be active. Eating three meals a day gives kids the energy they need.

fiber (FYE-ber): Fiber is the part of plant foods the body cannot break down. Fiber helps the digestive tract and heart.

hydrated (HYE-drayt-id): The body is hydrated when it has enough water. Staying hydrated is important for delivering vitamins and minerals throughout the body.

minerals (MIN-er-ulz): Minerals are naturally occurring substances that are good for the body. Minerals help the body fight illnesses and break down food into energy the body can use.

nutrients (NOO-tree-entz): Nutrients are substances the body needs to grow. Vitamins and minerals are nutrients.

vitamins (VYE-tuh-minz): Vitamins are substances that are important to the development of the body. For example, B vitamins help your body make energy.

whole grains (hol GRAYNZ): Whole grains contain all the nutrients in a grain seed. Fiber, minerals, and vitamins are found in whole grains.

To Learn More

BOOKS

Graimes, Nicola. *Kids' Fun and Healthy Cookbook.* New York: DK Press, 2007.

Swanson, Diane. *Burp! The Most Interesting Book You'll Ever Read about Eating.* New York: Scholastic, 2001.

WEB SITES

Visit our Web site for links about balanced meals: **childsworld.com/links**

Note to Parents, Teachers, and Librarians: We routinely verify our Web links to make sure they are safe and active sites. So encourage your readers to check them out!

Index